STONEHAM PUBLIC LIBRARY
431 MAIN STREET
STONEHAM, MA 02180

JAN 3 0 2017

W9-AHT-209

AVICENNA

LEADING PHYSICIAN AND PHILOSOPHER-SCIENTIST OF THE ISLAMIC GOLDEN AGE

PHYSICIANS, SCIENTISTS, AND MATHEMATICIANS
OF THE ISLAMIC WORLD™

AVICENNA

LEADING PHYSICIAN AND PHILOSOPHER-SCIENTIST OF THE ISLAMIC GOLDEN AGE

BRIDGET LIM
AND AISHA KHAN

ROSEN
PUBLISHING®

New York

Published in 2017 by The Rosen Publishing Group, Inc.
29 East 21st Street, New York, NY 10010

Copyright © 2017 by The Rosen Publishing Group, Inc.

First Edition

All rights reserved. No part of this book may be reproduced in any form
without permission in writing from the publisher, except by a reviewer.

Library of Congress Cataloging-in-Publication Data

Names: Lim, Bridget, author.
Title: Avicenna (Ibn Sina) / Bridget Lim and Aisha Khan.
Description: First Edition. | New York : Rosen Publishing, 2016. | Series:
  Physicians, scientists, and mathematicians of the Islamic world | Includes
  bibliographical references and index.
Identifiers: LCCN 2015047667 | ISBN 9781508171423 (library bound)
Subjects: LCSH: Avicenna, 980-1037.
Classification: LCC B751.Z7 L56 2016 | DDC 181/.5--dc23
LC record available at http://lccn.loc.gov/2015047667

Manufactured in China

CONTENTS

INTRODUCTION 6

CHAPTER ONE
THE GOLDEN AGE OF ISLAM 10

CHAPTER TWO
AVICENNA'S EARLY LIFE 27

CHAPTER THREE
ON THE PRINCE'S COURT 41

CHAPTER FOUR
PRINCE OF PHYSICIANS 58

CHAPTER FIVE
A SHORT LIFE WITH WIDTH 72

CHAPTER SIX
CHIEF OF THE WISE 84

TIMELINE 96

GLOSSARY 97

FOR MORE INFORMATION 101

FOR FURTHER READING 104

BIBLIOGRAPHY 106

INDEX 109

At a time when most of Europe was plunged in the "Dark Ages," the Arab world was experiencing a "Golden Age." Inspired by the writings of great Greek philosophers such as Plato and Aristotle, and the ancient writings of physicians such as Galen and Hippocrates, Muslim scholars tried to improve and apply their newfound knowledge to their own time and religious context.

Abu Ali al-Husain ibn Abdallah ibn Sina, or Avicenna as he is known in the West, was one such scholar. A medieval philosopher and scientist, he made enormous contributions to the fields of medicine, natural history, metaphysics, and religion. Avicenna was based in the Persian-speaking region of central Asia. Baghdad, the capital of the Islamic world, was an unparalleled center of learning. This was the golden age of Islam, a time when rulers funded the arts and sciences, and philosophers, artists, architects, and poets of all religions and ethnicities created a unique culture whose legacy is still cherished today. In today's world, Avicenna would have been called a prodigy—he had outpaced his teachers by the time he was fourteen years of age and was practicing medicine by the age of sixteen. He wrote his first book at twenty-one. As was the custom of the times, Avicenna

Abu Ali al-Husain ibn Abdallah ibn Sina, also known as Avicenna, was a renowned scholar in the Islamic world during the Middle Ages.

sought out royal patrons for his endeavors; as a result, he served sultans by day and pursued his personal scholarly interests by night.

Although Avicenna was curious about all branches of knowledge, his main concern was one that philosophers and scientists still ponder: the origin of the universe and of life. A devout Muslim, Avicenna sought to reconcile the rational science he had learned from the Greeks with the Islamic belief in a single, supreme god. His aim was to prove scientifically, or at least through reason and logic, that God exists and is the creator of the world.

Avicenna's use of Aristotelian logic and his work on the concept of "being" opened the door for a rationalist study of religion. Avicenna influenced the work of later Christian philosophers such as St. Thomas Aquinas, whose reasoning and conclusions predate the work of great Enlightenment thinkers of the eighteenth century such as René Descartes and Immanuel Kant.

But it is Avicenna's medical contributions for which he is most remembered. His monumental *Qanun fi'l-Tibb*, known as the *Canon of Medicine*, is regarded as possibly the greatest medical work ever. This one-million-word encyclopedia not only systematically presented all known medical knowledge, it also incorporated Avicenna's experiences and discoveries as a practicing physician. The *Canon* was available in a Latin translation in Europe one hundred years after Avicenna's death and continued to be used there for the next six centuries.

Avicenna's life was not one of mere book learning. As a practicing doctor and a political administrator, he incorporated his everyday observations into his work. His life was also marked by danger and intrigue. He was caught up in conflicts between petty rulers, and he even spent some time in prison, where he continued to write. He died while traveling at the age of fifty-eight, fleeing an army that had overrun his patron's kingdom.

Known as the "prince of physicians," Avicenna was a true Renaissance man—a person with a wide range of interests and expertise—centuries before the Renaissance ushered in a new era of scientific endeavor.

CHAPTER ONE

THE GOLDEN AGE OF ISLAM

Avicenna was born in 980 CE in Bukhara, Persia
(present-day Uzbekistan), during a unique time in the
Middle East. The relatively new religion of Islam had
spread outside Arabia and was extending its reach
into North Africa, Europe, and the rest of Asia. Muslim
Arabs were engaged in an exchange of goods and
ideas with very diverse peoples, a process that would
have a profound impact on Islamic culture and learning. It was in this dynamic and intellectual world that
Avicenna would find himself.

MUHAMMAD AND THE EMERGENCE OF ISLAM

Before Avicenna's birth, Islam emerged in the early
seventh century in the desert sands of Arabia. A forty-
year-old merchant named Muhammad (570–632), an

illiterate bedouin living in Mecca, announced that the
angel Gabriel had appeared before him to reveal the
word of God.

The revelation was radically different from the
beliefs and practices of the Arabs at the time.
Muhammad called on them to abandon their multiple
gods and idols and instead worship Allah, the one, true
God.

Muhammad also said that life was only temporary,
a short stop in the journey to an eternal life, which
would come after death. He said there would be a
day of judgment when all humanity would be resurrected and each person would have to answer to God.
On that day, those who had led a good, honest life,
remembering God and treating their fellow humans
with charity and dignity, would be rewarded with
heaven. Sinners would be sent to hell.

Islam has many similarities with Judaism and
Christianity, the two monotheistic faiths that preceded it. In fact, Muhammad (known to Muslims as
the Prophet) preached that he was the last in a long
line of prophets whom God had sent to show people
the right path, starting from Adam, through Moses
and Abraham, to Jesus. He urged Muslims to respect
their fellow "People of the Book" (those whose faith is
based on the divine revelations in the Torah and the

Bible) but said he had been chosen to deliver a new message because, over centuries, the teachings in the previous revelations had become distorted.

Muhammad received revelations for the next twenty years or so, until his death in 632. People memorized the revelations and wrote them on scraps of parchment and papyrus. After Muhammad's death, they were collected in a book called the Quran (also spelled Koran).

The powerful elite in Mecca, who made their living from the idol worship during the annual pilgrimages to the Kaaba shrine, were not pleased. Islam preached that everyone was equal, that status and respect were earned through good deeds and not inherited as a birthright. The elders turned violent, and Muhammad fled to the town of Medina in 622. The Muslim calendar begins from this year.

After many years of struggle and suppression, as well as three battles, Muhammad's teachings gained enough popularity that the elders of Mecca sur-rendered to his authority. He returned triumphant to his hometown in 632. By the time of his death later that year, Islam had spread throughout the Arabian Peninsula.

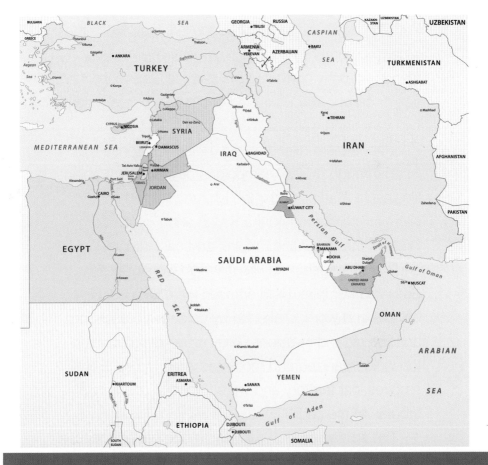

Islam spread throughout the eastern regions of central Asia after Muhammad's death in 632. Today, Islam is among the world's predominant religions. There are more than one billion Muslims living and worshipping around the world.

A STRING OF SUCCESSORS

With the death of the Prophet, the leading men in the Muslim community agreed on Muhammad's close friend and early convert, Abu Bakr, as his successor, or caliph. Abu Bakr died of natural causes within two years and was succeeded in 634 by Umar ibn Khattab, a stern ruler who expanded the frontiers of Islam through military campaigns beyond the Arabian Peninsula. Battles under Ibn Khattab helped spread Islam farther west, into the Syrian and Egyptian provinces of the Byzantine Empire, and east into Iraq and Persia (present-day Iran), which were under the Sassanian Empire. Both empires were long past their heights and were weakened by epidemics, declining agriculture, and invasions. They were little match for the well-organized and motivated Arab forces. Both empires lost territory and were forced to pay annual tributes to the caliph.

The spread of Arab rule was made easier because the vast majority of people cared little for who ruled over them. Many welcomed Arab rule because their taxes were lower and they were more remote. In addition, Muslim converts who learned Arabic had decreased the potential of obtaining a position within the new administration.

In Mecca, however, tensions between the dominant tribes were growing. The third caliph, Uthman ibn Affan, was accused of giving jobs to his own clan. A group emerged that claimed Ali, a cousin and son-in-law of Muhammad, should have been the first caliph. They said only direct descendants of Muhammad should rule the Muslim community and that Ali had been cheated of his right. This group led an uprising in 656, and in the ensuing rioting, Uthman was killed.

The elders of Mecca chose Ali as the fourth caliph. But some Muslims revolted against him, saying he wasn't acting fast enough against Uthman's killers. At the same time, the governor of Syria, Muawiyah ibn Abi Sufyan, challenged Ali for the caliphate. Unrest grew and finally Ali's army faced Muawiyah's in the Battle at Siffin. The battle was inconclusive and both parties agreed to arbitration, but a section of Ali's supporters withdrew, saying a divine right couldn't be put to human judgment. This group, known as the Khwarijites, murdered Ali in 661. Muawiyah wrested control of the caliphate.

At this point, a majority of Muslims agreed to Muawiyah's rule, preferring security to mayhem. These Muslims were known as Sunnis. Other Muslims, who believed that only descendants of the Prophet should rule, championed the cause of Ali's sons, Hasan and

Hussein. They came to be known as Shia Muslims or Shiites, and from then on they had their own line of religious leaders, known as imams.

Muawiyah shifted the capital to from Medina to Damascus, and his successors are known as the Umayyads. After a few turbulent decades, an era of relative peace came with the rule of Abd al-Malik. He had the Dome of the Rock built in Jerusalem, one of the first grand mosques in the distinct Islamic architectural style. He also established a uniform currency, expanded the postal system, and made Arabic the official language across the empire.

The capital in Damascus was closer to the Mediterranean and North Africa, leading to a fruitful cultural interaction. Arabs came into contact with Christian sects. In the east, they adopted the administrative structure of the Sassanian Empire, and many newly converted Sassanian functionaries began working for the Arab governors.

Through taxes and tributes, many Arabs gained untold wealth. They maintained luxurious lifestyles, opulent homes, and beautiful mosques. Many of them took to patronizing the arts and sciences, commissioning both artistic and philosophic endeavors. In the early period there was an emphasis on religious studies as scholars studied the Quran. This extensive study and interpretation was linked to the development of Islamic law, which involved extrapolation from written commentaries. Other emphasis was placed on literature, since the Arabian Peninsula had a rich literary history of pre-Islamic scholars who worked to systematize the Arabic language.

THE HOUSE OF WISDOM

In 750, a group who claimed direct descent from Abbas, the Prophet's uncle, overthrew the Umayyad Dynasty. They founded the Abbasid dynasty and soon moved the seat of power from Damascus to Baghdad.

Because the Baghdad region had been controlled by the Sassanian Empire and the Abbasid leaders adopted of its system of government, Persians came to hold high posts in the caliphate.

The Abbasid caliphs found themselves in a stronger position, economically and militarily, than their predecessors. They had more time and resources to promote religious, cultural, and educational pursuits.

By this time the Arabs had embraced Greek learning, which, though shunned in Europe by the Catholic Church, was flourishing in Alexandria, Egypt. The Nestorians, a Christian sect who spoke Syriac, had fled the Byzantine Empire and moved into Arab lands, bringing with them copies of Greek texts on philosophy and natural sciences.

In Persia, the Sassanians had established a school at Jundishapur where they gathered Indian, Christian, and Jewish scholars. This school helped assimilate Western mathematics, astronomy, and astrology into traditional Indian education.

Most Muslims were eager to partake in this sharing of knowledge. A famous saying of the prophet Muhammad exhorts all believers to seek knowledge, even if it means traveling to China—which was then on the edge of the known world for Arabs.

Some Muslims didn't think it was wise to adopt foreign learning; they were especially wary of applying Greek philosophical methods to Islamic thought. But one of the first great philosopher scientists of Islam, Yaqub ibn Ishaq al-Kindi, wrote in the ninth century, "We should not be ashamed to acknowledge truth and to assimilate it from whatever source it comes to us, even if it is brought to us from former generations and foreign peoples. For him who seeks the truth there is nothing of higher value than truth itself; it never cheapens or abases him who reaches for it, but ennobles and honors."

The victorious Muslim armies brought back more than books. When they conquered central Asia in 751

CE, they took more than twenty thousand Chinese prisoners to Samarqand. These Chinese knew how to make paper and gunpowder, and soon these technologies began to spread. The availability of paper helped speed up translation and writing.

The fourth Abbasid caliph, Harun ar-Rashid, began ruling in 786 CE. He established a library that housed works from across the empire. Harun also commissioned translations. He promoted Arabic literature, and scholars started compiling the tales of the famous *One Thousand and One Nights*, or *Arabian Nights* as it is more commonly known. He had diplomatic contacts with the West and sent King Charlemagne an elephant and a watch, then unknown in Europe.

This period is known as the golden age of Islam, when Baghdad was the center of culture and learning. Scholars and artists from across the known world traveled there to avail themselves of the support the caliphs showered on the arts and sciences.

Harun's son Mamun inherited his father's love of knowledge and he established the Bayt al-Hikmah (House of Wisdom), a library, translation center, academy, and observatory in 830 CE. Mamun gathered multilingual scholars to translate Greek, Persian, and Sanskrit texts and welcomed learned men. Musa al-Khwarizmi, the father of algebra (which got its name from the title of his book, *Kitab al-Jabr*), worked at the House of Wisdom. Another celebrated scholar was a Nestorian Christian, Hunayn ibn Ishaq, known in the west as Johannitius, who published many original works and commentaries. It was during this period that Al-Azhar University in Cairo and Damascus University in Syria were established, two centuries before the first university in Europe.

SCIENCE, MATHEMATICS, AND MEDICINE

Muslims were also making great strides in the sciences. It was at the House of Wisdom that Greek geometry met Indian arithmetic, resulting in the system of Arabic numerals (Arabs called them Hindu numbers) and the concept of zero, replacing the cumbersome Roman numerals. As noted earlier, al-Khwarizmi developed

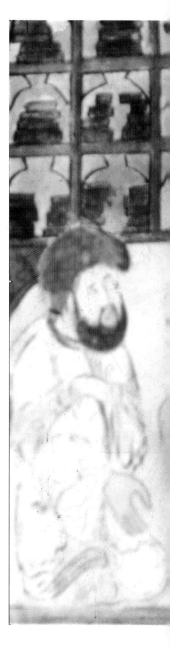

Many of the greatest minds of Islam's so-called Golden Age were residents of the House of Wisdom, or Bayt al-Hikmah, in Baghdad. These scholars translated classical Greek works into Arabic and also made original contributions to the fields of philosophy, mathematics, and the sciences.

JOHANNITIUS

One of the House of Wisdom's most important and prolific contributors was Hunayn ibn Ishaq al-Ibadi (808–873), a Nestorian Christian known in the West as Johannitius. He was probably from southern Persia. His native language was Syriac, but he was also fluent in Greek and Arabic and he began translating texts at the age of seventeen. Johannitius was a physician by education and he translated nearly all the Greek medical texts available at the time, including ninety-five Syriac and thirty-four Arabic versions of works by Galen.

Johannitius was the lead translator at the House of Wisdom and also served as chief physician to the caliph al-Mutawakkil. He wrote several original medical treatises as well as commentaries on the texts he translated.

As one of the pioneers in the translation movement, Johannitius was confronted with the difficult task of translating complex concepts from Greek to Arabic. Later scholars remark that he achieved a great degree of accuracy and sensitivity in his translations and helped establish new Arabic terms for philosophical, medical, and scientific concepts. His son Ishaq ibn Hunayn, who was equally gifted, followed in his footsteps.

Unfortunately, Johannitius's church was not pleased with some of his work and he was excommunicated. A deeply religious man, Johannitius was apparently devastated and committed suicide at the age of sixty-six.

algebra, including linear and quadratic equations, and applied it to contracts, land surveys, and tax collection. He also developed algorithms; this term is derived from his name.

Other mathematicians delved into binomials and polynomials. Concepts in geometry originally introduced by Euclid and Archimedes were further developed, laying the groundwork for the modern system that emerged centuries later. Arabs made advances in trigonometry, discovering the cosine, and developing the remaining trigonometric functions: sine, tangent, cotangent, secant, and cosecant. The needs of a growing empire and thriving trade also led to the innovation of double entry, a method of bookkeeping that is still used around the world.

Muslims were especially attracted to medical sciences. The Quran says God has a cure for every disease, and physicians were eager to find those cures. The Abbasids promoted medical learning, and hospitals were established with permanent endowments. The first was built in the 800s in Baghdad under Harun ar-Rashid. Within one hundred years, there were five other hospitals, or *bimaristans*, in Baghdad alone. In addition to general physicians, hospitals had ophthalmologists, surgeons, and bonesetters on staff. The government even sent doctors with traveling pharmacies to care for prisoners.

In applied chemistry, Muslims discovered better and more efficient ways for tanning leather and forging metals. They developed many compounds and substances, some medicinal. The names of many substances, such as alcohol camphor, borax, and elixir, are derived from Arabic.

Arabs also focused on astronomy, as it was important to determine the positions of heavenly bodies to know in which direction to pray toward Mecca. Arabs were also interested in maritime sciences since they used to sail to Africa, India, and Southeast Asia to trade. They tried to correct and refine Ptolemy's *Almagest*. Muslims used the mariners' compass and made improvements to the existing design of the astrolabe and typical nautical maps. Arab astronomers knew Earth was round and successfully calculated its circumference. It is possible that Abul Hasan Al-Ashari (Al-Haytham) invented the telescope, though some historians also note that the instrument may have been in use earlier by the ancient Greeks. Arab scientists invented the pendulum and also pioneered the use of hydraulic presses and water clocks, which tracked the passage of time and the phases of the moon.

اگر مسافت زیرین بود و شش ماه و جیوان و نبات بگی تلف شدی از غایت

حرارت و همچنین از رست راس اگر شش ماه دور و رست جیوان و نبات از

برودت هلاک شدی و سخن فلک آفتاب و آن مسافت، همین سطح اعلی سیم سفل

باشد ثلثانة الف و جمسه و جمسون الف و اربعه و سیصد و میلا و صورت او دونیت

آفتاب بزرگ کوکب است و سنجان کوبنید

کر آفتاب ملک که ابکت و قبروز و بره و عطار و کاتب و مربع صاحب چش

و مشتری قاهی و زحل صاحب خزان و زهره جبیا که و خدمتکار و افلاک

اقالیم و بروج شهره ها و درجات دهها و قایق تخلیا و توانی منازل و آیین سیه

خوبت و از عجایب لطف باری در جل و علا آفت کرآفتاب را و درفلک جیارم

Astronomy was an important field of study at the House of Wisdom and beyond, as this illustration of celestial orbits from an early Persian manuscript shows.

Abu Ali al-Hasan ibn al-Haytham (Alhazen) developed a theory of vision. In his *Book of Optics*, he takes a mathematical approach to understanding sight, reflection, and refraction of light and color. He also developed some of the principles on which the modern camera works and was the first to understand that the eye perceives images because of light rays emitted from the object.

CHAPTER TWO

AVICENNA'S EARLY LIFE

● ●

In the Islamic world of Avicenna's time, knowledge was pursued and passed on by men of faith. Since there were no formal religious institutions to teach Islamic theology and the Quran, students learned under the guidance of tutors. This study of Islam was considered a prerequisite to broader education.

Although little is known of the medieval Islamic scholars, we do have access to some information about Avicenna's early years in the form of a brief autobiographical sketch he dictated to his student Abu Ubayd al-Juzjani. It covers approximately the first thirty years of his life, up to the point he met al-Juzjani, who became his lifelong disciple and companion.

Avicenna was born into a Persian family in the village of Afshana, near Bukhara, in 980. His mother's name was Sitara (also spelled Sitareh), and his father, Abd Allah, a native of Balkh, was the governor of Kharmaithan, near Bukhara. After the birth of

Avicenna's younger brother five years later, their father moved the family to Bukhara so his sons would have greater opportunities. At the time, Bukhara was the administrative capital of the Samanid caliphate, the court under which Avicenna eventually worked.

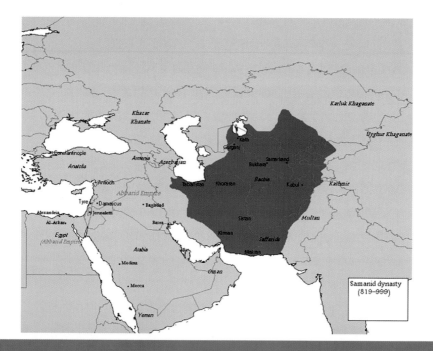

This map shows the reach of the Samanid dynasty until just a decade after Avicenna's birth. The Samanids were known for their emphasis on culture and intellect. However, the dynasty and its cultural revival would not last.

THE SAMANID DYNASTY

Central Asia had been under the influence of Islam for nearly one hundred years by the time Avicenna was born. The local rulers had generally accepted the supremacy of the caliphate in Baghdad but sometimes fought battles with each other.

The founder of the Samanid dynasty was Samankhoda (also spelled Khudat), a Persian convert to Islam who challenged the Tahirid rulers who had been battling Baghdad for dominance. Caliph al-Mamun rewarded Samankhoda's grandsons with the governorships of Samarqand, Fergana, Shash (all in present-day Uzbekistan), and Herat (in present-day Afghanistan).

One of Samankhoda's great-grandsons, Esmail, who ruled as caliph from 892 to 907, defeated the Tahirids and established himself in Bukhara. In so doing, he won the recognition of Caliph al-Mutadid, though he did not pay the yearly tribute expected of other vassal states.

By the ninth century, Bukhara had grown into an urban center from a group of villages clustered around an oasis on the Zarafshan River. It was a fertile region renowned for its fruit, including pomegranates, apricots, and cherries. It was a vibrant stop on the trade routes running from the Byzantine cities of Rome and Constantinople, through the Middle East, and on to China and even Russia.

The Samanids were Sunni Muslims who were tolerant of other Muslim sects, including Shiites, and people of other religions. They were Persian descendants and revived aspects of the Persian Sassanian Empire.

In an attempt to re-create the glories of ancient Persia, the Samanids revived Persian as the state language—written in Arabic script—and ushered in a cultural revival. They supported Arab and Persian poets, writers, and philosophers, and they collected books. The Samanids also sent emissaries to different kingdoms to meet intellectuals, encouraging them to make Bukhara their home. Samanid sultans commissioned scholarly works, including commentaries on the Koran, medical discoveries, astronomy, and geography.

By the time Avicenna was born in 980, the Samanids' grip was loosening on the outlying areas of their territory. They were soon powerless to stop revolts by local administrators. As time passed, the political climate in the region became more turbulent, as Avicenna would witness in his lifetime.

RELIGIOUS EDUCATION

Avicenna's father was a member of the ruling elite, and he was eager to give his son the best education possible. At that time, the finest education meant learning Arabic in order to read the Quran. The next steps in his education were the *hadith*, learning the sayings of Muhammad as recorded and passed down by his companions; followed by learning Islamic law (*sharia*); and jurisprudence (*fiqh*).

In his dictated memoir, Avicenna says, "I was put under teachers of the Quran and letter. By the time I was ten, I had mastered the Quran and a great deal of literature, so that I was marveled for my aptitude."

That Avicenna had mastered the Quran by memorizing it at such an early age is evidence of his amazing memory, an ability that would prove especially useful in later years when he was almost constantly on the road, moving from one town to another, without access to his books or manuscripts. During this time, Avicenna often wrote from memory.

Like the rulers of the time, Avicenna's family was likely Sunni, though some later critics have said they were Shiite. Avicenna studied the philosophy of Sunni law with the learned Hanafi scholar Ismail al-Zahid. This particular scholar, whose works shaped Hanafi,

Avicenna was born into a family that prized education and was in a position to acquire it. As a boy, the gifted student sat at the feet of many knowledgeable teachers. Avicenna learned Arabic so that he could read, and memorize, the Quran.

one of the four schools of thought in the Sunni sect (the other three schools are Shafi, Hanbali, and Maliki), was considered moderate. Islamic learning, as shaped by Hanafi, was a predominant teaching method in Bukhara during Avicenna's youth.

During Avicenna's youth, his father knew of the importance of mathematical methods unique to South Asia, for Indians were already using the decimal system and the concept of zero. An Indian grocer was hired to teach young Avicenna the system.

Avicenna grew up amid philosophical and religious discussions and an atmosphere of constant learning. He mentions his exposure to Shiite Ismaili philosophy, when his father entertained missionaries of the sect, but says that even at a young age he remained unconvinced.

PHILOSOPHY AND SCIENCE

It was clear that Avicenna was a gifted child. After he completed his religious studies, his father hired a philosophy and science teacher, Abu Abd Allah al-Natali, as a resident tutor. With him, Avicenna started his study of the Greek philosophical works through Arabic translations. According to Abu Nasr al-Farabi, another philosopher alive at this time, Avicenna began with a translation of the *Isagoge* by Porphyry, an introduction to Aristotle's *Organon*, the philosopher's collected works on logic theory of syllogisms. According to al-Farabi, Avicenna dictated in his autobiography, "[Al-Natali] was extremely amazed at me; whatever problem he posed I conceptualized better than he, so he advised my father against my taking up any occupation other than learning."

Through learning the philosophy of Sunni law, or *fiqh*, Avicenna had already been exposed to practical logic and deductive reasoning. Logic is the science that studies the principles and criteria of inference and demonstration, or the structure of arguments. Its aim is to distinguish between reasonable or poor arguments. Logic is often applied as a form of reasoning, consisting of a major premise, a minor premise, and a conclusion. For example, the statement *All humans are mortal* would be considered a major premise, while the statement *I am a human* would be considered a minor premise. Therefore, the conclusion to this argument is *I am mortal*. This three-point structure is known as a syllogism, a form of deduction that philosophers used to express universal truths. In order to test the validity of any theory, a philosopher examines its logic. If the premises are faulty, the inference is faulty, creating a fallacy.

A categorical syllogism contains precisely three terms: the major term, which is the predicate of the conclusion; the minor term, the subject of the conclusion; and the middle term, which appears in both premises but not in the conclusion. Thus one categorical syllogism could be: *All philosophers are men* (middle term); *all men are mortal*; therefore, *all philosophers* (minor term) *are mortal* (major term). Venn diagrams are a pictorial representation of categorical syllogisms. To make accurate syllogisms, it is necessary to classify everything in appropriate genera and subcategories. Thus, in the above argument, philosophers are categorized as humans. Humans can be a larger category of mammals and so on.

The middle term is considered the key to a syllogism, and it is considered the key to moving an argument forward. According to Avicenna, mastering this logic marks men of learning and higher ability from others.

Studying Aristotle's *Organon*, Avicenna stunned his teacher by taking an unconventional approach to the concept of genus and on how to isolate the middle terms.

After logic, al-Natali introduced Avicenna to mathematics through the works of Euclid and Ptolemy, walking him through the first few theorems and leaving him to read the rest himself. "Such autonomy is the mark of truth," Avicenna later wrote.

"Teaching provides only a hint of the problems, which the real intelligence solves for itself." This experience would color much of Avicenna's later philosophy. His book *Hayy ibn Yaqzan* (*The Living Son of the Vigilant*) chronicles how humans can reach the truth independently by describing how a child living alone on an island discovers God through nature. Avicenna's autobiography further emphasizes the importance of independent learning.

When al-Natali left Bukhara, Avicenna continued to read on his own. He studied various works on the natural sciences and philosophy. He read Aristotle's *Metaphysica*, but it made little sense to him at thirteen. He recalled reading it forty times, until he had it memorized but admitted that he still couldn't make out its true purpose. Still hungry for knowledge, Avicenna next turned to medicine.

MEDICINE

After he read works of philosophy and the sciences, Avicenna said, "Next, I desired to study medicine, and proceeded to read all the books that have been written on this subject." Arab medicine at that time was greatly

One of the great ancient Greek philosophers whom Avicenna studied was Aristotle. Aristotle was considered by many Muslim scholars to be the First Teacher. This means that they learned Aristotle's works and then interpreted them through their own Islamic belief system.

Rhazes is shown examining a young patient in this print. This Persian physician and philosopher had studied and improved upon Galen's scholarship. Avicenna, in turn, improved upon Rhazes's work.

influenced by Greek tradition. Avicenna pored over the translated works of both Hippocrates and Galen, who was physician to Marcus Aurelius. Galen's knowledge was adopted and improved by an array of scholarly physicians before Avicenna, including Yaqub ibn Ishaq al-Kindi and the great Persian physician Abu Bakr Muhammad ibn Zakariya al-Razi, known in the West as Rhazes.

Rhazes's most famous work is the nine-volume *Havi* (*The Virtuous Life*), a medical encyclopedia in which he wrote about new discoveries. He was the first to use alcohol as an antiseptic and made fine strings from animal intestines for sewing wounds. Al-Kindi was the first to write about the symptoms and treatment of smallpox and chickenpox.

Even though conflicts between Shiites and anti-Shiites continued, the Abbasids revered intellectualism and made time to expand libraries and centers of learning. They had established hospitals with teaching facilities where doctors practiced and taught. Rhazes headed the Muqtedari Hospital in Baghdad that maintained a well-rounded curriculum, in line with the concept that a truly learned man had more than one area of expertise. Pharmacology, or the study and identification of medicines, was highly developed and most hospitals had herb gardens and pharmacies.

The precocious Avicenna, who could not have been more than fifteen years of age at this time, said "Medicine is not a difficult science, and naturally I excelled in it at a very short time, so that qualified physicians began to read medicine with me."

Avicenna continued to practice medicine throughout his life. During good times he treated people for free. When he had no other means, he would make his livelihood from clinics he established, where he noted, "the methods of treatment derived from practical experience revealed themselves to me such [ways] as baffle description."

After studying medicine, Avicenna began rereading texts on philosophy and logic. During this time he claimed that he had not been sleeping through the night. If he felt sleepy or weak, he would drink coffee (referred to by Arabs at this time as "wine") to help him stay alert, or if he was trying to solve a particularly difficult problem, he would go to a mosque and pray until the answer came to him. But despite his ability as a philosopher, it was medicine that would open the next door in Avicenna's life.

CHAPTER THREE

ON THE PRINCE'S COURT

I n 998, Nuh ibn Mansur, Samanid prince of Bukhara, became gravely ill. None of his court physicians could cure him. Desperate, members of the prince's court recommended that Avicenna be summoned. Though still a teenager, Avicenna had earned a stunning reputation as a medical expert.

THE ROYAL LIBRARY

Avicenna attended to the prince, and soon he was cured. In return, the prince enrolled him as a court physician. After a while, as he gained the prince's confidence, Avicenna sought permission to enter the royal library. The library's huge collection of books on all subjects, from literature to philosophy to astronomy, rivaled that of Baghdad. Avicenna described it as a mansion filled with many chambers, each one filled with books on a particular subject. For Avicenna, it was as if someone had handed him the keys to the world. He spent the next year devouring the contents of Prince Mansur's library.

By the time Avicenna was eighteen, he had made his way through the library's storehouse of knowledge. "My memory for learning was at that period of my life better than it is now," he later said, "but today I am more mature; apart from this my knowledge is exactly the same, nothing further having been added to my store since then."

Soon after, the library was destroyed in a fire, and Avicenna's detractors—he already had many—accused him of setting the blaze so that he could attribute the contents of those books to himself. As a Persian with a

بعد وفاته على ولده ابي طالب رستم واجلسوه على تخت الملك وسـّروا الامارة وسـّريرا من الديوان الـ

واحد من هـولاء سنوردهـلـك موضعها انك الله تعالى ولما تزين تاج المملكة وتشرف سـرير السلط

When Avicenna provided the cure for the prince's ills, he was hired as court physician. Avicenna soaked up as much medical knowledge as he could. He also would become a confidant of the prince, an alliance that would prove important.

father who had dabbled with Shiite doctrine, Avicenna was an easy target.

Shortly after, at the request of a neighbor, Avicenna wrote the *Kitab al-Majmu*, or *The Compendium*, a book that covered all branches of knowledge except math. He was twenty-one, and soon after he was commissioned for two other works by a lawyer—one a commentary on legal matters called *Kitab al-Hasil w'al-Mahsul* (*Import and Substance*) and another was a work on ethics called *Kitab al-Birr w'al-Ithm* (*Good Work and Evil*).

INTERPRETING GREEK PHILOSOPHY THROUGH THE LENS OF ISLAM

As noted earlier, Avicenna was interested in metaphysics, having read Aristotle's *Metaphysica* but was unable to fully understand it. The information that Aristotle had presented became clearer to Avicenna shortly before he came into the service of Sultan Nuh ibn Mansur. He was on a booksellers' street when a vendor approached him with a copy of Abu Nasr al-Farabi's commentary on *Metaphysica*. Avicenna admits that at first he wasn't interested because of his futile experience with the original work, but the seller was persuasive and offered a great discount. Avicenna says he rushed home to read it, and it was as if all of Aristotle's intent was revealed to him. In gratitude, he says, he went out the next day to give charity to the poor.

Following the Aristotelian system, Avicenna understood that philosophy is the pursuit of all knowledge. Philosophy can be divided into practical applications such as the philosophy of economics, politics, and ethics and the more speculative pursuits, which included theology, mathematics, and physics. All six sciences have pure and applied aspects. Avicenna regarded theology as the most important of sciences because it involves the study of God and creation and unites all of the branches of learning, since everything leads back to the creator. In keeping with this philosophy, knowledge is the criterion by which souls will be judged in the afterlife.

Avicenna learned that Aristotle believed the principle governing the world was motion. Things were constantly in a state of change. Since everything in the universe was in motion, Aristotle regarded the universe as eternal. But there must be something that put it in motion. According to Aristotle, this prime mover was God. Plato, on the other hand, conceived of God as pure good or pure intellect. In Plato's opinion, God didn't create but rather emanated the universe, like the sun emits light. Plato thought that the objects in this world were imperfect copies of permanent forms that existed in an "intelligible" world.

Independent of the Greeks, Muslim theologians had built a collection of writings and opinions about God and creation that were derived from the Quran. They considered the Quran a miraculous revelation and proof of the existence of God. They debated questions about God and his attributes, fate, free will, and the afterlife. They examined whether the world was eternal or created and whether God controlled every individual occurrence in the universe. When faced with Greek rationalism, many theologians adopted a methodological argument to buttress their position, which is often called the Kalam school of thought.

Scholars in this tradition were called Mutakallimun (those who practice *kalam*, or discussion and debate) and their argument, to put it simply, was that it is clear that the world exists. And since the world exists, there must be something that caused it to exist, and that something is God. They recognized that this argument could be used to ask who made God, but they argued that this would create an infinite chain, which would be absurd. Instead, they said the chain stopped with God, who created the universe from nothing and controlled every aspect of it, from the stars to a falling leaf to every human action. Thus, the Mutakallimum

The Muslim philosopher al-Farabi was an important influence on Avicenna. His mastery and interpretation of Aristotle's great works helped Avicenna understand the ancient Greek's philosophy.

rejected the rational concept of cause and effect, since they believed that God caused everything, and they rejected a notion of natural laws.

But many Muslim scholars were taken by the Aristotelian emphasis on rationality and reason and the Neoplatonic school of thought derived from Plato.

The most important of these was Abu Nasr al-Farabi, who is regarded as one of the greatest of medieval Muslim philosophers, second only to Aristotle. Al-Farabi disagreed with the Mutakallimun and instead developed a concept of emanation. He argued that God is the First Being, from whom emerges the First Intellect. That First Intellect reflects on itself and, in doing so, produces the First Heaven and the Second Intellect. This process continues until the Tenth Intellect, which produces the moon and the earth. It was al-Farabi's work that helped unlock the full meaning of Aristotle's logic for Avicenna.

AVICENNA'S METAPHYSICAL WRITINGS

Avicenna dealt with metaphysics in several of his later works, most comprehensively in his *Kitab ash-Shifa* (*Book of Healing*), which was a compendium on several subjects that he wrote over twelve years.

In the sections on God, existence, and the human soul, Avicenna sought to reconcile his religious beliefs in God, whom the Quran describes as the creator of the worlds, with the rationalism and logical method he learned from the Greeks.

Avicenna begins the *Book of Healing* by stating, "there is no doubt that there is existence"—this is something humans know immediately, as a form of self-consciousness. Then he makes a distinction between forms of existence, arguing that we can imagine that nothing in this world exists. But if we try to imagine there is no cause for the world, we are unable to do so, since we know that the world exists and there has to be something that caused it to exist. This something is God. Avicenna calls God the "Necessary Being," since we cannot logically imagine a world without him. Everything else is merely "possible." That is, it need not have existed, but it does because God caused it to, and in that sense it is necessarily existent.

But this argument relied on man's intuitive abilities, and Avicenna also proposed to prove the rationality of God's existence and the universe. To do this, he presented a unique and important philosophical distinction between essence and existence.

Essence, for Avicenna, was the aggregate of the defining characteristics of a thing—living or inanimate.

I THINK, THEREFORE I AM

In his discussions of existence, and specifically the existence of a soul and consciousness, Avicenna put forth a unique idea. He said: "Imagine a man created all at one and in perfect bodily condition, but whose eyes are screened so as to prevent him from perceiving external things. Imagine further that this man floats in empty air [vacuum] in such a manner that he has no sensation, not even such as may be caused by the touch and friction of air." Such a man, Avicenna argued, will still be able to reflect upon himself and affirm his own existence, though he won't be able to prove he has a body or that anything other than his self-consciousness exists.

This concept is considered revolutionary because it foreshadowed one of the most important doctrines of the eighteenth-century period of Enlightenment, René Descartes's famous three words, *Cogito, ergo sum*— "I think, therefore I am." Descartes arrived at this conclusion because he rejected tradition and cast doubts upon everything. But to doubt one's own existence required thought, which in turn proves one's existence. This philosophy asserted humans as rational beings, giving prominence to the idea of mind over matter, or even the soul.

For example, "humanness" encompassed the characteristics that make a mammal a human. He distinguished this essence from existence, which is the addition of matter to an essence. So, all humans may not be alike, though they share the same essence. Further, Avicenna noted that it is possible to conceive of an essence without it having an existence because an essence itself cannot cause it. But there is one being whose essence cannot be contemplated without its actual existence, and that is God, because in Him, essence and existence are the same.

Avicenna weaved this notion of God as the Necessary Being with al-Farabi's system of emanation, but for Avicenna, the intellects are the archangels and the tenth (intellect) is the Active Intellect that gave rise to our earthly world, emanating souls and giving them form. These heavenly beings may cause things, but they cannot create something from nothing, as God can; they need matter on which to act. Avicenna also argued that although God caused the universe, it was eternal, emanating from God's self-knowledge, and was caused because it is an aspect of His essence.

This metaphysical structure allowed Avicenna to regard God as the creator, but a very remote creator: the being who started the universe but does not intervene in its functioning. Thus, Avicenna incorporated scientific principles and the rational concept of cause and effect with his religious beliefs. In keeping with this philosophy, although God is the ultimate creator of humankind, he does not predetermine the course of human life the way most Muslim scholars believed. Humans exercise free will within the boundaries of the laws of nature.

One modern scholar has described Avicenna's argument as a "creative evolution." Every new development is a possibility, but it occurs within limits set by the prior process of evolution.

Avicenna believed that through logic and reasoning, humans can grasp the underlying framework that governs this world and the being that led to its creation; thus humans can achieve knowledge of God. In fact, to Avicenna, understanding God was the ultimate realization of human potential and spirituality.

MOVING ON

Avicenna's father died when he was twenty-two years old. In his autobiography Avicenna said that he took an administrative post under the Samanid rulers, but around 999, he moved to Gurganj in Khiva (present-day Turkmenistan). It is possible that the same religious and racial tensions that had surfaced during

ICI CRIE DEX CIEL ET TERRE SOLEIL EC LVNE EC COR ELEMENZ

Avicenna saw a conflict in his belief, stemming from the Quran, that God was the creator of all things, and the rational logic of the ancient Greeks. In time, Avicenna devised a philosophical theory that reconciled God's existence with the scientific principles in which he also believed.

Abu Raihan Muhammad ibn Ahmad al-Biruni was an Islamic scholar who served on the courts of more than six caliphs. Like many of the great thinkers of the Islamic world's Golden Age, his quest for truth motivated him to seek knowledge through research and innovation.

the burning of the library may have forced him to leave Bukhara.

Turkic power was on the rise as could be witnessed with the growing influence of Sultan Mahmud of Ghazna. Mahmud later sought Avicenna for his court, but the scholar avoided him, fearing his capricious and violent temperament. Someone had even accused Avicenna as being a blasphemer because he believed the world was eternal and he denied that humans would be resurrected physically on the day of judgment.

Avicenna also denied that humans could define God. In Muslim tradition and in the Quran, God is known by various names including, Most Merciful, All-Knowing, and All-Powerful, but Avicenna believed that the names could not be taken literally, drawing the wrath of most traditionalists.

Still, the vizier of Gurganj, a learned man, was pleased to host Avicenna. He introduced him to the emir, Ali ibn Mamun, who gave him a position at his court with a handsome salary. It was in Gurganj that Avicenna met another great philosopher-scientist, Abu Raihan Muhammad ibn Ahmad al-Biruni. But Avicenna's stay in Gurganj was short-lived. Avicenna was forced to flee again, this time for reasons unknown, though historians have noted that Sultan Mahmud of Ghazni was infuriated by Avicenna's refusal to join his court. He ordered the emir to deliver Avicenna and several other courtiers, including al-Biruni, to Ghazni.

The emir let the scholars know of the sultan's intentions, giving them the choice of going with the sultan's men or escaping. Al-Biruni reluctantly chose to go to Ghazni, fearing Mahmud's wrath, but Avicenna and a Christian scholar, Abu Sahl 'Isa ibn Maymun ibn al-Masihi, decided to flee since they had heard of Mahmud's intolerance and traditional beliefs.

Mahmud was infuriated and sent out men to hunt them down; in fact, wanted posters were made featuring a portrait of Avicenna and distributed in the region. On the fourth day of his escape, he and al-Masihi got stuck in a sandstorm and his friend, unable to bear the heat, died of thirst.

Somehow Avicenna survived and eluded his hunters, traveling from town to town with the goal of reaching Jurjan (present-day Iran at the southeastern end of the Caspian Sea). He wanted to enter the service of Gunbad-i-Qabus, the emir noted for his love of learning. But by the time he got to Jurjan, Qabus had been overthrown and imprisoned, where he was starved to death. Avicenna kept traveling, but he eventually returned to Jurjan where he met his lifelong friend Abu Ubaid al-Juzjani.

Avicenna soon found himself in a vexing situation. Because he had become so famous due to his scholarship, at least one leader was willing to have him kidnapped. Yet others were unwilling to hire him for fear of angering Mahmud. Upon considering his predicament, he composed the following couplet:

And great once I became, no more would Egypt have me,
And when my value rose, no one would care to buy me.

CHAPTER FOUR

PRINCE OF PHYSICIANS

· ·

Al-Juzjani recounted that in Jurjan, a wealthy noble
by the name of Abu Muhammad al-Shirazi bought
Avicenna a house where he again turned his attentions
to medicine. In order to earn a living, Avicenna began
treating patients on a regular basis. He also continued
his independent studying and teaching. Avicenna's
student and scribe al-Juzjani visited him every day,
to hear his lectures on logic and to read Ptolemy's
Almagest. It was here that Avicenna, on the constant
goading of al-Juzjani, began writing the *Canon*, the
medical encyclopedia that would seal his fame as the
"prince of physicians."

THE LADY

Soon after, Avicenna moved to the small principality of
Rayy (near present-day Tehran, Iran). The ruler of Rayy
was Majid ud-Daulah, but in reality, the power behind

the throne was his mother, al-Saiyyida, or "the Lady." She had assumed power on her husband's death because Majid was a minor. Even when he came of age, she refused to hand over the throne.

Avicenna established a successful clinic and also offered his services at the royal court, where he was quickly welcomed. Majid was suffering from depression, probably because of his lack of influence, and Avicenna succeeded in alleviating his condition.

After two or three years, Majid's own brother, Shams ud-Daulah, ruler of Hamadan, attacked the city over the killing of an official.

By this time, Avicenna had managed to anger al-Saiyyida by giving his honest opinion that she should hand over power to Majid, who was the legitimate heir. Unwelcome in Rayy, Avicenna again chose to flee.

AVICENNA WRITES A FIVE-VOLUME CANON

As Avicenna compiled the *Canon*, a book of more than a million words in five volumes, he wrote, "Medicine is the science by which we learn the various states of the human body in health, when not in health, the means by which health is likely to be lost, and when lost, is likely to be restored to health."

Avicenna's *Canon of Medicine* was an astounding achievement. In five volumes, Avicenna compiled a comprehensive study of medical information known to scholars at that time. The *Canon* was so esteemed that it was used as a medical textbook for centuries.

Book one of the *Canon* deals with the basic principles of medicine, drawing heavily on the early Greek traditions. It discusses the four elements—earth, water, air, and fire—and the four bodily fluids—yellow bile, black bile, blood, and phlegm. The latter were the four humors that were believed to govern a person's temperament. It was thought that good health depended on maintaining a balance between these humors. In addition, every substance was believed to have either a hot or cold property. Because it was believed that diseases caused an imbalance in these humors, physicians had to identify the imbalances and offer medicine, food, and care that would restore the patient's harmony.

Book one of the *Canon* also includes information related to human anatomy and the causes, symptoms, and treatments of diseases. Avicenna also discusses preventive measures and emphasizes the importance of good hygiene in the *Canon*, where he wrote, "As long as the air is good and clean and not mixed by anything which is incompatible with the patient's temperament, health will materialize."

The second volume of the *Canon* includes more than seven hundred medicinal plants and substances and for many centuries was the most comprehensive source of medicinal substances available. The third volume examines in detail diseases that affect particular parts of the body. The fourth volume explains various symptoms and diseases that affect the body as a whole, such as fevers, poisoning, and rashes, as well as wounds and fractures. Avicenna again returned to the importance of hygiene, emphasizing the need to take care of hair, skin, nails, and body odor. It is in this section that he discusses problems and solutions for underweight and overweight persons.

Avicenna also discusses psychological and emotional factors that affect health and related illnesses such as depression. He spoke of lovesickness, for which he prescribed uniting the pining person with the object of his or her desire. He also believed that music could have a positive effect on persons of compromised health.

Volume five discusses how to mix substances to make medicines and in what doses to administer them. Avicenna believed in experimentation. He offered seven rules for testing drugs and advised testing them

The foundation of the entire work of the *Canon* is Avicenna's theory about the four elements of the cosmos: fire, water, earth, and air. His belief that germs could be transmitted through the elements was groundbreaking.

on animals to determine their effects. Avicenna's seven rules remain remarkably close to today's modern drug trials.

Avicenna combined his book learning with his clinical experience in order to write the *Canon*. And even though most of his clinical notes were lost by the time he sat down to compose the encyclopedia, he was able to rely on his legendary memory for extremely accurate descriptions.

Although Avicenna generally remained influenced by Greek medicine, he wasn't afraid to challenge its premises, as he did when he explained that a person could die from excessive blood to the head—such as from brain hemorrhages and tumors—which the ancients thought impossible. He was the first physician to say that tuberculosis was contagious, and centuries later he was proved correct.

Avicenna was also the first physician to recognize that germs can be transmitted through air, water, or soil, noting "at certain times the air becomes infected and anyone breathing the infected air falls sick." He even said that the cause was tiny organisms that travel through air or water, a fact only verified centuries later through the invention of microscopes and the germ theory of disease. He correctly wrote that ancylostomiasis (hookworm infection) was caused by intestinal worms.

Avicenna also described meningitis, and he devoted attention to gynecological problems and to proper childcare. He performed surgeries and is said to have worn green robes while operating. He also developed surgical instruments, including a probe for the eye.

THE BOOK OF HEALING

After falling out of favor in Rayy, Avicenna made his way to Hamadan, where he was eventually summoned to the court of Prince Shams ul-Daulah to treat him for colic. He stayed in the palace for forty days, earning the gratitude and favor of the prince, who gave him a position at his court.

The philosopher accompanied the prince on his military campaigns, as an advisor and physician, and he was soon given the post of vizier, or prime minister.

But the army turned against him (al-Juzjani hinted that they thought Avicenna might expose their corruption). In a sort of mini coup the soldiers surrounded his house, hauled him off to prison, and ransacked his belongings. They even tried to get him executed, but the sultan drew the line at that, instead banishing him from Hamadan. Avicenna went into hiding at the home of a friend.

AN EARLY TAKE ON CANCER

Avicenna believed that cancers were caused by an excess of black bile, which contributed to excessive heat in the body. He said a benign tumor could be differentiated from a cancerous one by certain symptoms such as pain, throbbing, and rapid growth. He also noted that cancerous tumors send out "crablike tracks" and occurred more often in hollow organs, which is why they were most common in women. Avicenna also stated that cancers often strike muscles, tendons, and lymph nodes.

He said a cure was most likely if the cancer was caught at its earliest stages. The first goal should be to halt the cancerous growth. Avicenna recommended surgical removal if the tumor was small and accessible and not close to major organs. If it "can be arrested with anything, it can be so by vigorous excision ... including all the [blood] vessels supplying the tumor so that nothing of these will be left." He also advised that surgery be preceded by purifying the body of excess black bile. This could be achieved by providing a nutritious and balanced diet to the patient to maintain purity and strengthen his or her organs. In advanced cases, Avicenna advised against excision, saying the tumor would only grow back.

However, the prince fell ill again and summoned Avicenna, whose medical skills returned him to favorable health. The prince apologized for what had transpired and appointed him vizier once again.

Around the same time, al-Juzjani had been pleading with Avicenna to write a commentary on Aristotle, but the philosopher, who was busy with matters of state, said he didn't have the time. Finally, Avicenna agreed, saying, "If you will be satisfied for me to compose a book setting forth the parts of those sciences which I believe to be sound, not disputing therein with any opponents no troubling to reply to their arguments, I will gladly do so." And that was how he began work on the *Kitab ash-Shifa*, or the *Book of Healing*.

Avicenna was a man of great energy and purpose. He rose before dawn for the first prayers of the day and then wrote for several hours. Later, when his pupils joined him, he discussed his recent passages with them. After a brief period of study, Avicenna began his duties as vizier where he dealt with administrative matters until noon.

He then returned home for lunch, at which time he usually had guests. After eating and socializing, Avicenna usually took a brief rest and later attended to the prince and his court. Avicenna returned home by sunset, where after dinner, he would have another

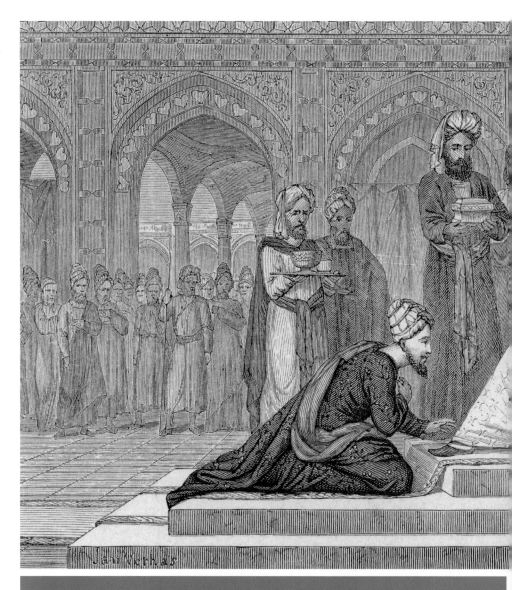

Shams ul-Daulah appointed Avicenna to the office of vizier on his court. As vizier, Avicenna was a high-ranking political adviser, or minister, to the emir. This was a tenuous position, however, and it ended at Shams ul-Daulah's death.

study session with his students, giving lectures and dictating notes for his books. In the evening they drank wine and were entertained by court musicians (music was another of Avicenna's passions). Among orthodox Muslims of the time, Avicenna's love of wine and music provoked consternation, and he was also faulted for his odd hours and active love life and social schedule.

WRITING IN HIDING

Avicenna's structured court life did not last. After a few years, Prince Shams ul-Daulah fell ill while on a military expedition. His soldiers rushed to bring him back to Avicenna, carrying him in a cradle, but he died on the way. The prince's son, Sama ud-Daulah, was installed as emir, and the army asked Avicenna to stay on at his post as vizier. But Avicenna refused, probably wary of the people who had almost killed him years earlier.

Avicenna went into hiding and wrote to Shams's brother, Ala ud-Daulah, emir of Isfahan, seeking a post within his court. In the meantime, at al-Juzjani's prodding, he continued work on his *Book of Healing*. Since he didn't have access to books, he wrote entirely from memory. He drew up a framework and then systematically filled in each topic from a range that included natural sciences (except zoology). Al-Juzjani claimed that he wrote fifty pages every day.

At this time, a search was under way for Avicenna, as the sultan's deputy suspected him of intrigue with Ala ud-Daulah. Betrayed by an enemy, Avicenna was caught and then imprisoned in a fortress called Fardjan where he spent four months. He wrote a couplet:

> My going in was sure, as you have seen
> My going out is what many will doubt.

In prison, he wrote the *Kitab al-Hidaya* (*Book of Guidance*), *Hayy ibn Yaqzan* (*The Living Son of the Vigilant*), and a treatise on colic; he had written the

Cardiac Remedies earlier. As described earlier, *Hayy ibn Yaqzan* is the tale of a man who grows up alone on an isolated island, yet through sheer intuition, intellect, and reasoning is able to arrive at ultimate truths about reality, being, and God. It is a parable that explains Avicenna's view of knowledge as both intuitive and rational. According to Avicenna, it is through a logical thought process that a connection with the Active Intellect may be formed. This connection is what unveils the mysteries of the universe.

Soon after Avicenna was imprisoned, Ala ud-Daulah attacked and captured Hamadan, and Sultan Ali and his minister were placed in the same fortress as Avicenna. Having secured their submission, Ala ud-Daulah freed them and allowed Ali to retain nominal authority. Avicenna was released too, and he took lodgings at the house of a friend.

CHAPTER FIVE

A SHORT LIFE WITH WIDTH

· ·

Avicenna fled Hamadan in disguise, along with al-Juzjani, his brother, and two slaves. The men wore thick woolen robes so that they would appear to be Sufis, Muslim mystics. They headed to the court of Ala ud-Daulah, patron of scholars. After many hardships, they reached Isfahan, and Ala ud-Daulah and other notables came out to greet them. "At court he was received with the respect and consideration that he so richly merited," wrote al-Juzjani.

Every Friday night, Ala ud-Daulah would gather all the scholars in his court for learned discussions, where Avicenna dazzled his peers and provoked much envy. It was here that the philosopher set about completing the *Book of Healing* and several other works.

AVICENNA'S TREATMENT OF THE NATURAL SCIENCES

Like the *Canon*, the *Book of Healing* is also an encyclopedia, but it deals mostly with metaphysics, mathematics, astronomy, and the natural sciences. Avicenna greatly valued the pursuit of knowledge because he believed that it was only through reasoning that humans could perfect their immortal souls. He was convinced that it was only through the pursuit of learning that man could come into contact with the Active Intellect, the tenth celestial entity. For Avicenna, this was the purpose of human life, to experience the divine spark that caused our world. He also believed that knowledge was the sole criterion by which humans would be judged in the afterlife.

Among humans, Avicenna regarded prophets as the most intellectually developed. He believed they had the strongest intuition since they had pure souls and were in contact with the Active Intellect, which gave them divine revelations.

Since the concepts of metaphysics in the *Book of Healing* were discussed earlier, let's now consider its treatment of the natural sciences. Avicenna believed in both observation and experimentation (which was shunned as impure science by Aristotle). Once, when a meteor fell in the region, Avicenna examined it closely and proceeded to melt it to see whether or not it was metallic. The *Book of Healing* also included detailed descriptions of natural phenomena such as rainbows and geological formations including descriptions of igneous and sedimentary rocks and stalagmites, with references to Avicenna's own childhood observations of the Oxus River (the present-day Amu Darya River) in Bukhara.

Avicenna devoted special attention to physics, and the study of motion, which Aristotle considered the governing principle of the universe. He realized the problems with Aristotle's theory of projectile motion and theorized a concept of inertia. He also argued that when an object is set into motion, it retains some of that energy and that energy would not dissipate in a vacuum. Avicenna attempted to calculate this force mathematically, considering that the motion

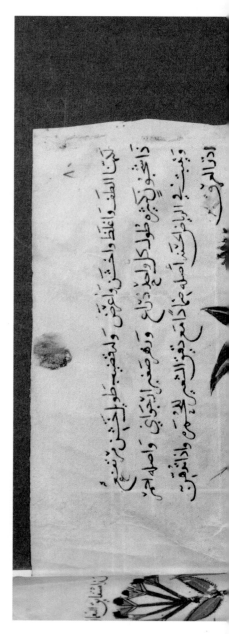

Avicenna believed in the use of plants and herbs as elements of healing. He routinely distilled essential oils from natural plants to treat a variety of ailments. Though not used extensively in the West, plant-based medicines are widely accepted courses of treatment in other parts of the world. This image has been shifted 90 degrees in order to show the plants more clearly.

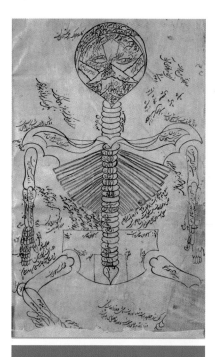

Avicenna's *The Canon of Medicine* contains remarkably detailed illustrations of the skeletal system.

of an object would be inversely proportional to its weight, giving birth to a rudimentary concept of momentum—the product of mass and velocity.

Avicenna also discussed various procedures for purifying metals in the *Book of Healing*. And he rejected the concept of alchemy—the centuries-old hunt for a substance, sometimes called the "philosopher's stone," that would turn ordinary metals into gold. He declared alchemy unscientific and futile and also rejected astrology, writing that it was impossible to say what influence the stars have on our lives.

Avicenna discussed the animal kingdom, focusing mostly on humans. He improved the Aristotelian system by incorporating new information on human anatomy, especially of the female reproductive system and the role of male and female "semen" in reproduction. Aristotle had refused to believe that there were ovaries or female "semen." Avicenna accepted the existence of ovaries but clung to the incorrect belief that women cannot have more than a passive role in the development of the fetus.

Avicenna also wrote several treatises on the eye, its structure and functioning, and ocular diseases, which were a special concern in the desert lands of Arabia and central Asia. In his discussion of sight, Avicenna breaks with Aristotle, who believed the eye issued some sort of ray toward objects it saw, and argued that the objects themselves send off rays to the eye. He also argued that sight occurred through the nerves, and not the "crystalline" globe.

As previously mentioned, Avicenna loved music, which was considered a part of mathematics in ancient times. Avicenna's main contributions to math are in the field of music, although he also composed original compositions.

In a short time Avicenna became one of the Ala ud-Daulah's close aides. He held no official position, but he was an esteemed advisor and accompanied the sultan on his journeys and wars. On one such trip, Ala ud-Daulah expressed dissatisfaction with astronomi-cal tables and he commissioned Avicenna to update them. Al-Juzjani helped the philosopher select instru-ments and workers, and they proceeded to tabulate more accurate measurements.

It seems from his vast accomplishments that Avicenna was indefatigable. Al-Juzjani narrates an incident in which a messenger brought a note to a pupil of the philosopher from a certain judge in Shiraz, in southern Persia. The judge objected to some arguments Avicenna had made in an essay on logic that he had incorporated in his *Kitab al-Najat*, or *Book of Deliverance*. The student handed the note at the end of a long summer day. Avicenna read it and immediately called for ink and paper. And while his friends and disciples sat around talking and eventually fell asleep, Avicenna wrote all night, drafting an immediate reply. In the morning he handed the response, some fifty sheets, to al-Juzjani to give to the messenger, saying, "I made haste to reply so that the messenger should not be delayed."

BOOK OF WISDOM FOR ALA

It was with Ala ud-Daulah that Avicenna found true respect and support. And in honor of his patron, he composed two works in Persian, which was the sultan's (and Avicenna's) native language.

The more important one is the *Danesh-Nama e Alai*, or *Book of Wisdom for Ala*. In the preface, he wishes his benefactor "all his wishes, in security, and eminence

and honor" and notes that in this "prince's shadow
I have achieved all ambition—for security, dignity,
respect for science."

The *Danesh-Nama* is a concise primer on philosophy, written for a layperson, that includes sections
about logic, metaphysics, math, and science. Experts
have remarked on its graceful conversational style,
its humor and wit, and the ease with which Avicenna
transfers complex ideas and terms from Arabic to
lively, colloquial Persian.

But alas, Avicenna's final days were less than
peaceful. Sultan Mahmud, who had been the scourge
of the Abbasids, was again flexing his muscle in
Transoxania. Al-Saiyyida of Rayy had died, and her
son, Majid, finally had his chance on the throne.
Unfortunately, he proved an inept ruler and invited
Mahmud to help him in his battle with a neighbor. The
Ghaznavids took the opportunity to seize Rayy and
unleashed a wave of persecution against various sects
and ethnic groups.

Ala ud-Daulah tried his best to placate Mahmud,
but he eventually sent his son to attack Isfahan in
1030. Ala ud-Daulah fled when the Turkish army
entered the city, and Avicenna likely left with him.
His home in Isfahan was looted and his books were
taken to Ghazni. Many of his works were lost forever,

WILLING TO LEARN

In his biography of Avicenna, al-Juzjani narrated an incident that gives us an idea about Avicenna's keen intellect and competitive streak. A question related to philology (the study of literature) arose during a discussion in front of the sultan in which Avicenna also gave his opinion. But one scholar, Abu Mansur al-Jabban, turned to him and said, "You are a philosopher and a wise man, but you have never studied philology to such an extent that we should be pleased to hear you discourse on the subject."

Avicenna was stung by this and devoted the next three years to studying the subject, sending for books from far and wide. When he was satisfied, he composed three odes of rare expression in the style of three different authors. He had the works bound as a book with the title smudged and presented it to Abu Mansur with the comment, "We found this volume in the desert while hunting, and you must look it through and tell us what it contains."

Abu Mansur examined the book and was baffled by some of the passages. Avicenna then innocently remarked that if he were to read certain books on philology he would understand everything. Abu Mansur then realized that Avicenna was the author and apologized profusely for his prior insults.

including the *Kitab al-Insaf* (*Book of Impartial Judgment Between the Easterners and Westerners*) of which only fragments survive.

THE END

It was during this time that Avicenna fell ill with colic. It was a severe attack, and he gave himself strong medicines. To make matters worse, he was on the road with the sultan, fleeing the Ghaznavid army. He gave himself injections, but one his servants gave him an overdose of a medicine that made him worse. Al-Juzjani hinted that the servants may have attempted to poison Avicenna on purpose, possibly because they had stolen from him. Avicenna was taken back to Isfahan where his condition stabilized enough for him to continue to accompany Ala ud-Daulah in battle again. Avicenna's condition deteriorated again and he stopped treating himself, saying, "the manager who used to manage me, is incapable of managing me any longer so there is no use trying to cure my illness." Avicenna died soon after in Hamadan, in 1037, at the age of fifty-seven. He had always said, "I [prefer] a short life with width to a narrow one with length."

Avicenna was not a particularly popular man in his own lifetime. Although he was a devout Muslim, he lived an unconventional lifestyle and had many unconventional views. He never married but was certainly not celibate. Many of his works went against the mainstream Muslim religious thinking at the time and he was often accused of being a *kafir*—or a "heretic." Allegations of being a closet Shiite followed him his entire life. Defending himself, he once said, "If I am a heretic, then there is not a single Muslim anywhere in the world." By many historical accounts, Avicenna was of striking good looks. He wasn't falsely modest; he

Avicenna is entombed in Hamadan, Iran. He died in 1037, at the age of fifty-seven. The accomplished scholar had lived a rich life full of intellectual pursuits that continued to resonate long after he was gone.

could be arrogant and scornful of mediocre intellects, sometimes ridiculing others' scholarly work.

Throughout history, critics have sometimes spread derogatory rumors about Avicenna; he was even occasionally portrayed after his death as an evil sorcerer. His detractors also liked remarking that the great physician was unable to heal himself. Nonetheless, Avicenna continues to have an impact on science and philosophy today.

CHIEF OF THE WISE

Despite living in such politically turbulent times, in permanent exile from his native land and forced to flee from one city to the next, Avicenna led a productive life. He was active in politics and government; he was a practicing physician and a renowned philosopher. He wrote hundreds of treatises, and more than two hundred of his works still survive, most remaining unstudied in detail.

In his lifetime, Avicenna had a mixed reception. For many philosophers who worked within the Greek tradition, Avicenna was a great commentator and elucidator of Aristotelian thought. He provided Muslim, Christian, and Jewish scholars a means to adapt the rationalist Greek methodology to their monotheistic faiths. For physicians, he was the final word and for philosophers, a foundation on which to build their theories.

But traditional religious theologians, both Christian and Muslim, sometimes rejected Avicenna. They believed that Avicenna was a heretic because he had adopted pagan Greek logic and appeared to limit God's powers. The notion that Greek-inspired metaphysics, and even sciences, was ungodly was beginning to strengthen, and several caliphs and Christian kings banned or executed philosophers who were considered irreligious.

In the East, the Abbasid Empire was fragmenting, and traditionalism and rigidity were taking hold in Arab lands that had once been the centers of experimental learning. Even in faraway Spain, where Muslim rulers had created a cosmopolitan haven for scientists and philosophers, European attacks were taking their toll.

But ironically, in the Islamic world, Avicenna's metaphysical theories were ultimately eroded because of the criticisms of two philosophers, both schooled in the Greek, but with opposing views.

CRITICISM OF HIS WORK

Nearly fifty years after Avicenna's death, Abu Hamid al-Ghazali took issue with the Greek-influenced Muslim philosophers. Since Avicenna was the most important thinker of this group, al-Ghazali focused his study and criticism on Avicenna's work.

What is unique about al-Ghazali's critique is that because he was trained in Greek logic and methods, his analysis is a rational examination of what he thought were the contradictions in Avicenna's metaphysical system. In his *Incoherence of the Philosophers*, al-Ghazali listed twenty features of the *falasifa*'s thought, of which only three went against both religion and logic. In fact, al-Ghazali felt that the philosophers, in their eagerness to adopt Aristotle, had rejected or mangled parts of their religion that they needn't have.

The first contradiction, according to al-Ghazali, is the *falasifa*'s belief that the universe is eternal, emanating instantaneously from God's self-reflection. Al-Ghazali challenged the belief that if God is logically the only Necessary Being, the universe had to come *after* him, both in time and being, and therefore cannot be truly eternal. Second, al-Ghazali disagreed with Avicenna's belief that God only governs universals, not individual human actions. He says there is no contradiction in the chain of causality to accept God's knowledge of all details. Finally, al-Ghazali disagreed with Avicenna's rejection of bodily resurrection, arguing that since God is the Necessary Cause, it is not

Avicenna was commemorated on a Soviet postage stamp in the 1970s. The fact that he was remembered nearly one thousand years after his birth proves the long-lasting contributions Avicenna made to philosophy, the sciences, and medicine.

Averroes's comprehensive commentaries on Aristotle put him in a unique position to analyze Avicenna's interpretations.

impossible for him to give the resurrected souls bodies in the afterlife.

Almost a century later, another great philosopher, Abul-Walid ibn Rushd, known in the West as Averroes, took issue with al-Ghazali and also with Avicenna. In his response to al-Ghazali, which he titled *Incoherence of the Incoherence*, Averroes argued that there was no incompatibility between religion and philosophy if both were understood soundly. By that time, Averroes had access to better translations of the Greek works and he blamed the confusion about the apparent contradictions between Aristotle and Islam on Avicenna, saying that the latter had misrepresented the Greek's thought in his attempt to mesh religion and reason.

At the same time, Averroes admired Avicenna's contributions to medicine and wrote a book examining a poem Avicenna had crafted, the "Urjuza fi'l-Tibb"

("Poem on Medicine"), which served as a memory aid to students of the *Canon*.

Despite criticisms, Avicenna remained a respected figure in the Arab-speaking world for his accomplishments in both medicine and philosophy. He was alled the *Sheikh al Rais* (Chief of the Wise, or Third Teacher), after Aristotle and al-Farabi.

Gerard of Cremona's translation of Avicenna's *Canon* in the twelfth century brought a whole new audience to the work.

AVICENNA'S LEGACY

At the turn of the millennium, as Europeans conquered parts of Muslim Spain, they came into contact with the works of al-Farabi, Avicenna, Averroes, and others and through them the works of Aristotle and Plato. When the city of Toledo was captured, they found a translation bureau similar to the Bayt al-Hikmah, where multilingual Christian, Jewish, and Muslim scholars were working together to translate books into Hebrew

Avicenna's scholarship on metaphysics influenced later generations of intellectuals. In the eternal quest to reconcile faith with reason, Catholic priest Thomas Aquinas used Avicenna's arguments to form his own proof of the existence of God.

and Latin but chiefly Arabic, which was the international language of science and philosophy.

In the West, the Church had mostly banned the study of the Greeks, regarding them as pagans, and the original works written in Greek were lost. But the Arab efforts, especially Avicenna's, to adapt and reconcile Greek thought within a religious framework opened the door for a new Western interest in Aristotle and the other Greek philosophers. This eventually led to the Renaissance and the Enlightenment.

The new Christian rulers took over the bureau in Toledo and began translating the Arabic works into Latin. Many Europeans learned Arabic in order to read the translations of Aristotle and others as well as the *falasifa*'s commentaries and the new medical and scientific treatises. Jewish scholars, who had found peace and security in Muslim lands, were at the forefront of this work, playing the role the Syrian Christians had three centuries earlier.

One of the most influential translators was Gerard of Cremona. Known as the "Master," Gerard translated seventy-one works from Arabic, including translations of Aristotle and Avicenna's *Canon* and the *Kitab ash-Shifa* (*Book of Healing*), which was called the *Sufficienta*.

The *Canon* soon became the standard textbook throughout Europe. The oldest existing Western syllabus, at the famous School of Medicine at Montpellier, lists the *Canon*. The text continued to be used well into the seventeenth century. Medical students learned Arabic in order to study it.

Eventually, of course, medical advances made many aspects of the *Canon* outdated. But Avicenna can be credited with connecting the medical system of Hippocrates and Galen with modern medicine.

In the field of philosophy, Avicenna's metaphysics was to have a profound effect on the medieval Scholastics—Christian theologians who, freshly exposed to Aristotle and Plato, took on the same task as the Muslim *falasifa*, to reconcile reason with faith. The most important of these scholars, St. Thomas Aquinas, used Avicenna's arguments to build his own rational proof of the existence of God.

Aquinas accepted Avicenna's distinction between essence and existence and the concept of necessary and being. But Aquinas further developed the concept of a theory of causal relationships that better fit with rational science. Although, as Christian, he accepted that everything other than God was possible, he also stated that God created things in such a way that they became the cause of the actions they performed.

Avicenna studied Aristotle's writings on the soul and formulated his own philosophy. While imprisoned, he wrote the famous "Floating Man" treatise to prove the existence of the soul. In "Floating Man," Avicenna argues that the soul is both substantial and independent of the body.

Aquinas disagreed with Avicenna's attempt to prove that the universe was both created and eternal, saying that though it was possible, it was impossible to prove it.

During this time, Avicenna's philosophical reputation was tarnished when some other writers' works were wrongly attributed to him and some of his own works were poorly translated. During this time, the rumblings of the Renaissance were becoming stronger. Leonardo da Vinci rejected the *Canon*, finding it outdated in the natural sciences, but he still used the Arabic terms, since there was no other terminology at the time.

Avicenna's influence, both in the West and East, has survived many interpretations. For example, Muslim Sufis and Christian religious sects, including the Franciscans, saw his theory of emanation and his emphasis on uniting the soul with its maker as opening the way for a mystical love for the divine, with God shining his light on mankind through the Active Intellect.

Scholars today, both in the West and in the Muslim world, continue to review Avicenna's works, many of which have not yet been subjected to a detailed examination. His medical treatises, especially on herbal cures, still guide natural healers, and his philosophical treatises still help illuminate man's most puzzling questions.

Avicenna is revered as one of the greatest minds of all time—a man with unlimited interests, an insatiable curiosity, and deep, profound appreciation of the mystery of life.

Today's physicists are still in search of a "unified theory," something that will encompass the workings of all natural forces and give them a clue to the origin of the universe. In a sense, Avicenna sought to do the same, as he was looking for a way to understand the universe based on concrete laws of cause and effect and a wise, loving God. According to his biographer, he said, "The heart of learning is a direct insight into the rational principles on which the world is constructed."

TIMELINE

476 Year given by historians to signify the end of the Roman Empire.

570 Birth of the prophet Muhammad in Mecca.

610 Muhammad receives the first revelations.

632 Muhammad dies.

660 Muslim armies conquer Egypt and Persia.

661 Muslims split into Shia and Sunni sects.

698 Muslim armies conquer North Africa.

719 The Iberian Peninsula is under Muslim control.

750 The Umayyad dynasty is overthrown by the Abbasid dynasty; Abbasid capital is moved to Baghdad.

760 Arab scholars adopt Indian number system.

768 Unification of the Roman Empire under Charlemagne.

786 Reign of the fourth Abbasid caliph Harun ar-Rashid.

830 The House of Wisdom is built in Baghdad.

980 Avicenna (Ibn Sina) is born in Persia.

998 Avicenna cures the Samanid sultan of Bukhara, Nuh ibn Mansur.

999 The sultan's library is destroyed by fire. Avicenna flees Bukhara and travels to Gurganj in Khiva (Turkmenistan).

1020 Avicenna is imprisoned in a fortress in Fardjan for four months.

1022 Avicenna leaves Hamadan and travels to Isfahan.

1037 Avicenna becomes ill from colic and dies.

abase To lower in rank or office.

alchemy A medieval chemical science that studied the convergence of base metals into gold.

Allah The Arabic term for "God" or "The Only God."

arbitration The act of mediating in order to settle a dispute.

assimilate To take in; to understand.

bedouin Member of a nomadic Arab tribe.

Byzantine Empire The eastern half of the Roman Empire, which survived for one thousand years after the fall of Rome. Its name comes from Byzantium, the original name of its capital city Constantinople. It declined when the Islamic Turks finally captured Constantinople in 1453.

caliph The title given to Muhammad's successors. The Umayyad rulers of al-Andalus claimed the title in 929, although many Muslims disputed their right to it.

capricious Impulsive.

colic A sharp, acute pain in the abdomen.

colloquial Relating to informal conversation.

coup A brilliant, sudden, or unusual stroke or act.

devout Deeply religious or devoted.

emanate To come forth from a source.

emir The Arabic word for an important noble who ruled a large region; it could mean "governor" but as these rulers were generally independent, it is probably best to translate it as "prince"; also spelled "amir."

endowment A gift or provision, usually to a person or organization that has proven its worth to society.

Enlightenment A philosophical movement of the eighteenth century that rejected traditional religious, political, and social ideas and ushered in an era of rationalism.

excommunicate To exclude from membership in a church by a religious authority.

exile Forced or voluntary removal from one's own country or kingdom.

extrapolation The inference of unknown information from known information.

Five Pillars The core beliefs of Islam, consisting of submission to Allah, prayer, fasting, charity, and pilgrimage to Mecca.

Galen The Greek-speaking Roman citizen whose systemization of Hippocrates's work would be the main medical technique in Europe and the Middle East for more than one thousand years.

heretic A person who holds different religious beliefs from those that are established and widely accepted.

hijra The Arabic term for the flight from Mecca to Medina by the Prophet Muhammad and his followers in 622. The Islamic calendar is reckoned from this date.

Hippocrates The ancient Greek physician and healer who laid the foundations of modern medicine.

indefatigable Untiring; tireless.

inertia The tendency of a body to remain at rest or continue in motion unless it is disturbed by another force.

Islam The Muslim religion, which includes faith in Muhammad as the prophet of God, or Allah. The name means "submission (to God)."

jurisprudence The science or philosophy of law.

Kaaba The large, black, cube-shaped shrine in Mecca; the holiest Islamic shrine. Millions of pilgrims visit Mecca every year.

kafir A heretic.

Mecca A city in central Arabia, the birthplace of Muhammad, and the holiest place in the Islamic world; all Muslims are supposed to pray in its direction five times a day.

metaphysics Philosophy that encompasses the nature of reality and being.

methodology A system of principles and procedures applied to a science or discipline.

monotheistic Belief in one all-powerful god.

Moors The name given to the Berber peoples of North Africa by the Spanish.

mosque A Muslim house of worship.

Muhammad The prophet of Islam. Born in Mecca, he lived from 571 to 632.

Muslim A follower of Islam.

opulent Abundant, lavish.

pagan A person who worships many gods.

Persia An ancient empire in the Middle East, occupying the region now called Iraq.

philology The study of language.

premise A proposition upon which an argument is based or from which a conclusion is drawn.

prodigy A child with exceptional talent.

profound Extending to or coming from a great depth; deep.

Quran The holy book of Islam (sometimes spelled Koran). Muslims believe that it was dictated to the prophet Muhammad by the angel Gabriel.

Shia A large sect of Muslims that separated from the Sunnis after the assassination of Ali. Shia Muslims constitute the majority in present-day Iraq and Iran.

sultan Ruler of a Muslim country.

Sunni The largest sect of Islam. Sunni Muslims reject the Shiite claim that Ali was the rightful successor to Muhammad. Most Arabic and African Muslims are Sunni.

syllabus The summary or outline that describes the content taught and the texts used during a college or university class.

syllogism A formal argument consisting of a major premise and a minor premise leading to a conclusion.

Syriac A literary language based on Aramaic and used by Christian sects.

tribute Regular payment from one state or ruler to another.

Umayyad A dynasty of caliphs that ruled the Muslim world until 750. A lone survivor of the dynasty reached Spain, where his successors would rule until 1036.

vassal A person in a subservient or subordinate position.

vizier Arabic title meaning prime minister; the most important official at the court of an emir.

Arab Science and Technology Foundation
P.O. Box 2668
Sharjah, United Arab Emirates
Website: http://www.astf.net
The Arab Science and Technology Foundation is an
    independent, nonprofit, non-governmental
    organization that works regionally and
    internationally to encourage investment in science
    and technology.

Center for Islamic Sciences
349-52252 Range Road 215
Sherwood Park, AB T8E 1B7
Canada
Website: http://www.cis-ca.org
The Center for Islamic Sciences promotes Islamic
    tradition of learning by establishing institutions of
    learning (schools, colleges, and research centers)
    for the promotion of Islamic tradition of learning
    and scholarship.

International Society for the History of Islamic Medicine
    (ISHIM)
P.O. Box 239
Manama
Kingdom of Bahrain
Website: http://www.ishim.net

The mission of ISHIM is to promote public awareness of the contributions of Arab and Muslim physicians to the history of medicine. The organization achieves this through encouraging more research and academic studies of earlier Islamic medicine, public outreach, and the establishment of a museum.

Metropolitan Museum of Modern Art
1000 Fifth Avenue
New York, NY 10028
(212) 535-7710
Website: http://www.metmuseum.org
The Metropolitan Museum of Modern Art features a collection of artifacts related to astronomy and astrology in the medieval Islamic world.

Museum of Science and Technology in Islam
4700 King Abdullah University of Science & Technology
Thuwal Jeddah 23955-6900
Kingdom of Saudi Arabia
Website: http://museum.kaust.edu.sa
This museum is part of King Abdullah University of Science and Technology. It explores Islamic contributions to science and technology.

U.S. National Library of Medicine (History of Medicine Division)
Building 38, Room 1E-21

8600 Rockville Pike
Bethesda, MD 20894
(301) 402-8878
Website: http://www.nlm.nih.gov
The world's largest biomedical library, NLM maintains
and makes available a vast print collection and
produces electronic information resources on a
wide range of topics that are searched billions of
times each year by millions of people around the
globe.

WEBSITES

Because of the changing nature of Internet links,
Rosen Publishing has developed an online list of web-
sites related to the subject of this book. This site is
updated regularly. Please use this link to access this
list:

http://www.rosenlinks.com/PSMI/avicen

Adamson, Peter. *Interpreting Avicenna*. Cambridge, England: Cambridge University Press, 2013.

Albert, Edouardo. *Ibn Sina: A Concise Life*. Leicestershire, England: Kube Publishing, 2013.

Al-Khalili, Jim. *The House of Wisdom: How Arabic Science Saved Ancient Knowledge and Gave Us the Renaissance*. New York, NY: Penguin Press, 2011.

Al-Khalili, Jim. *Pathfinders: The Golden Age of Arabic Science*. London, England: Penguin, 2012.

Avicenna, and Shams Constantine Inati. *Ibn Sina's Remarks and Admonitions*. New York, NY: Columbia University Press, 2014.

Barber, Nicola. *Medieval Medicine*. Chicago, IL: Raintree, 2013.

Belting, Hans. *Florence and Baghdad: Renaissance Art and Arab Science*. Cambridge, MA: Belknap Press of Harvard University Press, 2011.

Bobrick, Benson. *The Caliph's Splendor: Islam and the West in the Golden Age of Baghdad*. New York, NY: Simon & Schuster, 2012.

Freely, John. *Light from the East: How the Science of Medieval Islam Helped to Shape the Western World*. New York, NY: Palgrave Macmillan, 2011.

Fuess, Albrecht, and Jan-Peter Hartung. *Court Cultures in the Muslim World: Seventh to Nineteenth Centuries*. New York, NY: Routledge, 2011.

Kaukua, Jari. *Self-awareness in Islamic Philosophy: Avicenna and Beyond.* Cambridge, England: Cambridge University Press, 2015.

Lapidus, Ira M. *A History of Islamic Societies.* New York, NY: Cambridge University Press, 2014.

Nardo, Don. *The Birth of Islam.* Greensboro, NC: Morgan Reynolds Publishing, 2012.

Romanek, Trudee. *Science, Medicine, and Math in the Early Islamic World.* New York, NY: Crabtree Publishing Company, 2012.

Ruthven, Malise. *Islam: A Very Short Introduction.* New York, NY: Oxford University Press, 2012.

Saliba, George. *Islamic Science and the Making of the European Renaissance.* Cambridge, MA: MIT Press, 2011.

Scherer, Lauri S. *Islam.* Detroit, MI: Greenhaven Press, 2012.

Sharaf al-Din, Fatimah, and Intilaq Muhammad 'Ali. *The Amazing Discoveries of Ibn Sina.* Toronto, ON: Groundwood Books, 2015.

Siraisi, Nancy G. *Avicenna in Renaissance Italy.* Princeton, NJ: Princeton University Press, 2014.

Urvoy, Dominique. *Ibn Rushd (Averroes).* New York, NY: Routledge, 2015.

BIBLIOGRAPHY

Arberry, A.J. *Avicenna on Theology.* Westport, CT:
    Hyperion Press, 1979.
Bearman, P.J., et. al., ed. *Encyclopaedia of Islam.* "Ibn Sina."
    Leiden, Neth.: Brill Academic Publishers, 2000.
Berjak, Rafik, and Muzaffar Iqbal. "Ibn Sina: Al-Biruni
    Correspondence." *Islam and Science,* June 2003
    (http://www.findarticles.com/p/articles/mi_
    m0QYQ/is_1_1/ai_n6145344).
Carroll, William E. "Aquinas on Creation and the
    Metaphysical Foundations of Science." Notre Dame
    University (http://www.nd.edu/Departments/
    Maritain/ti98/carroll.htm).
Carroll, William E. "God Physics: From Hawking to
    Avicenna." Islamic Philosophy Online (http://www
    .muslimphilosophy.com/sina/art/gpa.doc).
Carroll, William E. "Thomas Aquinas and Big Bang
    Cosmology." Notre Dame University (http://www.
    nd.edu/Departments/Maritain/ti/carroll.htm).
Chishti, Hakim G. M. *The Traditional Healer's Handbook:
    A Classic Guide to the Medicine of Avicenna.*
    Rochester, VT: Healing Arts Press, 1988.
Dunn, Peter M. "Avicenna (AD 980–1037) and Arabic
    perinatal medicine." *Archives of Disease in
    Childhood Online,* July 1997 (http://fn.bmjjournals
    .com/cgi/content/full/77/1/F75).
Encyclopædia Britannica Online. "al-Kindi, Ya'qub ibn
    Ishaq as-Sabah" (http://search.eb.com/eb/
    article?tocId=9045485).

Encyclopædia Britannica Online. "Arts, Islamic" (http://
search.eb.com/eb/article?tocId=13717).

Encyclopædia Britannica Online. "Avicenna" (http://
search.eb.com/eb/article?tocId=9011433).

Encyclopædia Britannica Online. "Kalam" (http://search.
eb.com/eb/article?tocId=9044375).

Encyclopædia Britannica Online. "Logic" (http://search
.eb.com/eb/article?tocId=9110686).

Encyclopædia Britannica Online. "Metaphysics" (http://
search.eb.com/eb/article?tocId=9108718).

Fakhry, Majid. *A History of Islamic Philosophy.* New York,
NY: Columbia University Press, 1983.

Gohlman, William E. *Life of Ibn Sina*, New York, NY:
State University of New York, 1974.

Goodman, L. E. *Avicenna.* London,England: Routledge,
1995.

Hayes, John, ed. *The Genius of Arab Civilization.*
Cambridge, MA: MIT Press, 1983.

Hourani, Albert. *A History of the Arab Peoples.* New York,
NY: Warner Books, 1992.

Houser, Rollen E. "Avicenna, *Aliqui,* and the Thomistic
Doctrine of Creation" (http://www.stthom.edu/
houser/avicenna2000.pdf).

Leaman, Oliver. "Islamic Philosophy." In *Routledge
Encyclopedia of Philosophy,* edited by E. Craig.
London, UK: Routledge (http://www.rep.routledge.
com/article/H057).

Marmura, Michael E. "Avicenna on Causal Priority." In
Islamic Philosophy and Mysticism, edited by Parviz
Morewedge. New York, NY: Caravan Books, 1981

(http://www.muslimphilosophy.com/sina/art
/marmura4.pdf).

Nasr, Seyyed Hossein. *Science and Civilization in Islam*.
New York, NY: New American Library, 1968.

Nasr, Seyyed Hossein. *Three Muslim Sages*. New York,
NY: Caravan Books, 1976.

Rafael, George. "A Is for Arabs." Salon.com (http://www
.salon.com/books/feature/2002/01/08/alphabet
/index.html).

Sharif, M. M., ed. *A History of Muslim Philosophy*.
Lahore, Pakistan: Pakistan Philosophical
Congress, 1961 (http://www.muslimphilosophy.
com/hmp/default.htm).

Whitaker, Brian. "Centuries in the House of Wisdom."
Guardian, September 23, 2004
(http://www.guardian.co.uk/life/feature/
story/0,13026,1310285,00.html).

Wickens, G. M. *Avicenna: Scientist and Philosopher, a
Millenary Symposium*. London, England: Luzac
and Co., 1952.

Winter, H.J.J. *The Life and Thought of Avicenna*.
Bangalore, India: Indian Institute of Culture, 1952.

Yarshater, Ehsan, ed. *Encyclopedia Iranica*. "Avicenna."
New York: Routledge, 1982 (www.iranica.com).

INDEX

A

Ala ud-Daulah, 72, 77, 78, 79, 81
Arabic language, 16, 22, 24, 31, 91, 94
Aristotle, 6, 34, 35, 36, 44–45, 48, 67, 73, 74, 76, 77, 84, 86, 88, 89, 91
astronomy, 24, 77
Averroes, 88–89
Avicenna
   Canon of Medicine, 8–9, 58, 59–65, 72, 89, 91, 92, 94
   criticism of work, 85–89
   death of, 9, 81–83
   early life and education, 27–40
   full name, 6
   influence/legacy of, 8–9, 83, 84–85, 89–95
   metaphysical writings, 48–52, 73, 85, 92
   patrons of, 8, 41–45, 52, 55–56, 58–59, 65, 67–69, 72, 77, 78–79, 81
   practicing medicine, 6, 8–9, 40, 41, 58, 59, 65, 66
   in prison, 9, 65, 70, 71
   religion and, 8, 33, 40, 45, 49, 51–52, 55, 81–82

B

Baghdad, 6, 17, 19, 23, 29, 39, 41
Book of Healing (Kitab ash-Shifa), 48–49, 67, 70, 72, 73–76, 91
Book of Wisdom for Ala (Danesh-Nama e Alai), 78–79

C

Canon of Medicine (Qanun fi'l-Tibb), 8–9, 58, 59–65, 72, 89, 91, 92, 94

G

Ghazali al-, Abu Hamid, 85–88
Greeks, ancient, 6, 8, 17–18,

22, 24, 35, 36, 39,
44–46, 49, 61, 64, 84,
85, 86, 88, 91

H

House of Wisdom, 19–20,
22

I

Islam
  emergence of, 10–16
  golden age of, 6, 17–26
  spread of, 10, 12, 14,
    18–19

J

Johannitius, 20, 22
Juzjani Al-, 27, 56, 58, 65,
  67, 70, 72, 77, 78, 80,
  81

M

Mahmud of Ghazni, 55–56,
  57, 79
mathematics, 20–23, 33,
  35–36
medicine, 23–24, 36–40
Muhammad (Prophet),
  10–12, 14, 15, 17, 18, 31

S

Samanids, 28, 29–30, 41, 52

ABOUT THE AUTHORS

Bridget Lim has taught history and religion at the high school level. Currently, she is pursuing a Ph.D. in Islamic studies.

Aisha Khan is a journalist from India.

PHOTO CREDITS

Cover Everett Historical/Shutterstock.com; cover (background), pp. 3, 22, 50, 66, 80 gfxmart/Shutterstock.com; p. 5 Iqbal Khatri/Moment/Getty Images; pp. 6-7 kickimages/E/Getty Images; pp. 7 (inset), 89 Courtesy of the National Library of Medicine; p. 13 Rainer Lesniewski/Shutterstock.com; pp. 20-21 Print Collector/Hulton Archive/Getty Images; p. 25 Kharbine-Tapabor/The Art Archive at Art Resource, NY; p. 28 Arab League/Wikimedia/File:Samanid dynasty (819-999).GIF/Public Domain; p. 32 bpk, Berlin/Bibliotheque Nationale, Paris, France/Art Resource, NY; p. 37 DEA Picture Library/De Agostini/Getty Images; pp. 38, 60-61, 76 Wellcome Library, London; pp. 42-43 Edinburgh University Library, Scotland/With kind permission of the University of Edinburgh/Bridgeman Images; p. 47 © Art Directors & TRIP/Alamy Stock Photo; p. 53 SuperStock; p. 54 IgorGolovniov/Shutterstock.com; p. 63 Bibliotheque Mazarine, Paris, France/Archives Charmet/Bridgeman Images; pp. 68-69 © Mary Evans Picture Library/Alamy Stock Photo; pp. 74-75 Bibliotheque Nationale, Paris, France/Archives Charmet/Bridgeman Images; p. 82 Vladimir Melnik/Shutterstock.com; p. 87 Oleg Golovnev/Shutterstock.com; p. 88 Pictures from History/Bridgeman Images; p. 90 Renata Sedmakova/Shutterstock.com; p. 93 Bibliotheque Sainte- Genevieve, Paris, France/Archives Charmet/Bridgeman Images; additional cover and interior background patterns and textures javarman/Shutterstock.com, Dragana Jokmanovic/Shutterstock.com; back cover pattern MaryMo/Shutterstock.com

Designer: Michael Moy; Editor: Christine Poolos;
Photo Researcher: Nicole DiMella